THE FABULOUS FIESTAS OF THE PHILIPPINES

a seek and find book

by: Alexandra Romualdez Broekman

A SHORT INTRODUCTION TO the PHILIPPINES

The Philippines is a country in South East Asia. It is an archipelago - made up of more than 7,600 islands, surrounded by water.

It is very close to the equator, and is a tropical country. That means it is warm almost all year round, and many fruits, vegetables, and wild animals - especially in the ocean - live and thrive.

The Philippines got its name from the Spanish, who came to the land almost 600 years ago. They named it Las Islas Felipinas, after Prince Phillip II of Spain.

Though there had been other settlers before the Spanish, it was the Spaniards who stayed to rule over the Filipino people for over 300 years.

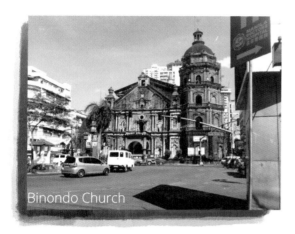
Binondo Church

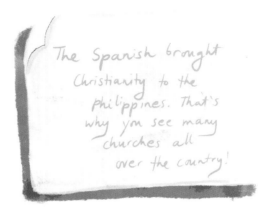
The Spanish brought Christianity to the Philippines. That's why you see many churches all over the country!

In 1898, the Philippines fought for independence from Spain, and although they were freed, the Americans then took over, and occupied the country for another 50 years. They stayed in power until just after World War II. Then, finally, the Filipinos were free from colonization, and were able to establish themselves as an independent nation.

Fort Bonifacio, Global City

View of Makati, Global City, and more

These days, the Philippines is known for many things: from the wide-ranging creative talents of Filipino artists and performers (such as Lea Salonga - famous for her work with Disney, and on Broadway), to the pristine sands of Filipino beaches (like Boracay).

Anilao, Batangas

Sunset over Manila Bay

As you go through the pages of this book, may you seek more knowledge of the Philippines, and find more joy and pride in knowing this unique, beautiful country better!

Chocolate Hills, Bohol

Mt. Mayon Volcano

ATI-ATIHAN

The Ati-Atihan is sometimes called the "Mother of all festivals" in the Philippines. The name, "Ati-Atihan" comes from the word "Aeta" - the first settlers of Panay Island.

The fiesta was once used to celebrate the "Barter of Panay" - when the Aeta accepted gifts from the Datu. The Datu were chieftains from Borneo who fled to Panay with their families to escape from tyranny in their own home. The Aeta gave them shelter in Panay, and in return received gifts. After converting to Christianity, the Church changed its meaning to celebrate the Santo Niño (the Holy Child/Child Jesus). During the festival, there is much dancing and holding of the statue of the Santo Niño.

The festival has begun! Can you spot these Filipino icons?

- a Philippine flag
- the stars and sun of the Philippine flag
- the map of the Philippines
- a mango
- a Philippine eagle
- an anahaw leaf

Some facts about the things you've just found...

	Philippine Flag	The Philippine flag was first used on June 12, 1898. The white triangle means liberty, fraternity, equality.
	Stars and Sun of the flag	The stars and sun are found on the flag and represent the 3 main islands (Luzon, Visayas, Mindanao) and 8 primary provinces.
	the map of the Philippines	The Philippines is an archipelago with over 7,000 islands! The many dots around the larger islands are many smaller islands.
	a mango	The mango is the National Fruit of the Philippines
	a Philippine eagle	The Philippine Eagle is the National Bird of the Philippines
	an Anahaw leaf	The Anahaw is the National Leaf of the Philippines

The 3 National Icons mentioned above are part of the official 12 National Symbols of the Philippines.

SINULOG

Where:
Cebu City, and Carmen City in Cebu Province
When:
3rd and 4th Sundays of January

The Sinulog Fesitval is one of the biggest celebrations in the Philippines. It attracts 1 to 2 million people to Cebu to join in the festivities every year. It is related to the Ati-Atihan, as it also celebrates the Holy Child (the Santo Niño), and Cebu City's fiesta even occurs on the same day as the Ati-Atihan (the 3rd Sunday of January).

The festival began officially in 1981, and is different from the Ati-Atihan because it also involves representatives from other provinces.

The festival involves a large parade, dances while holding and celebrating the Santo Niño, and street parties.

As we celebrate Sinulog, can you spot these stylish traditional Filipino garments and accessories?

Barong Tagalog

Baro't saya

Salakot

Pamaypay Abaniko

Terno

Bakyâ

Some facts about the garments and accessories you've just found...

	Barong Tagalog	The Barong Tagalog is a dress shirt often worn by men. It is usually made of Pineapple (pinya) fibers, and embroidered in a neutral color
	Salakot	The Salakot is a woven hat most popularly used by farmers
	Terno	The terno is a classic Filipiniana dress famous for its tall, stiff "butterfly sleeves"
	Baro't Saya	The Baro't Saya is the traditional national women's garb. It usually has a woven skirt with matching textile worn at the shoulder
	Pamaypay Abaniko	The Abaniko is a popular woven fan (hand-held) It is used as an accessory but also to beat the heat!
	Bakya	Bakya are traditional heeled wooden slippers

PANAGBENGA

The Panagbenga is a festival that happens every year in Baguio.

It begins on the 1st of February and goes for the whole month.

It is a celebration of flowers, and the blooming season. The festival began after the 1990 earthquake that caused much devastation across the big island of Luzon.

The parades, floats, blooms, flowers, and dancing symbolize "rising up" from the disaster.

The dances performed, and costumes worn highlight the indigenous cultures of the Cordilleras.

Visayan spotted deer

Palawan Flying Fox

Tamaraw

Tarsier

As the fantastic Panagbenga floats go by,
can you spot the native Filipino fauna hiding
amongst the flora?

Dugong

Whale
Shark

Some facts about the animals you've just found...

Many of the animals featured here are endangered? As citizens of the Earth, it's partly our responsibility to learn more about them, respect them, and protect them!

Visayan Spotted Deer	This deer lives only in the forests of the Philippines. They are nocturnal, and are considered endangered.
Tamaraw	The tamaraw is a small buffalo that is from the island of Mindoro. There are only around 500 tamaraws left in the Philippines (and the world).
Palawan Flying Fox	The Palawan Flying Fox is not a fox at all! It's a giant fruit bat that just LOOKS like a fox. They are found in - you guessed it, Palawan!
Tarsier	The Tarsier is one of the smallest primates in the world. They are found around Southeast Asia.
Dugong	The Dugong is one of 3 kinds of manatees (sea cows)
Whale Shark	The whale shark is the largest fish in the world! They get as big as a bus! They're known as the gentle giants of the deep

PAHIYAS

Where:
Lucban, Quezon

When:
Mid-May (around May 15)

The Pahiyas Festival is a harvest festival. It is known as one of the most colorful festivals in the Philippines.

The word "Pahiyas" actually comes from "payas" - which means to decorate.

The festival is a modernization of the celebrations hundreds of years ago when farmers would offer their harvests at the foot of the mountain.

Nowadays, the people of Lucban decorate their homes and streets with colorful flowers and fresh crops in acts of joy and thanksgiving.

During Pahiyas, whole homes and buildings lining streets are covered with fruits, vegetables, and flowers.

Can you spy these popular tropical fruits in this home's decorations?

 pineapple

 a branch of bananas

 atis

 mangosteen

 rambutan

 a bunch of lanzones

Some trivia about the fruits you've just found...

pineapple	The Philippines is one of the top 3 countries that produce and export this sweet, tart fruit to the world!
bananas	There are dozens of kinds of bananas! And the Philippines is one of the Top 5 producers and exporters!
atis	The Atis is also known as sweetsop or custard apple. It was first brought to the country by Spanish traders and colonizers from South America.
mangosteen	Mangosteen are famous for their hard, purple skin, but are actually soft, white, and sweet on the inside!
rambutan	In Malay/Indonesian the name "rambutan" is related to the word for hair: rambut. It does look like a hairy fruit!
lanzones	Lanzones are edible fruits grown off a variety of Mahogany trees from Southeast Asia

KADAYAWAN

The Kadayawan Festival is a Thanksgiving festival held every year in Davao City. It is a modernized celebration that harks back to when tribes would perform their thanksgiving rituals at the foot of Mount Apo.

These days, this days-long (sometimes even weeks-long) fiesta involves street dancing (Indak-Indak), floral parades (Pamulak), a beauty pageant (Hiyas ng Kadayawan), and even markets to showcase Davao's best farmed crops. In particular, the famous Davao durian is a highlight.

What famous Filipino food can you spot at the Kadayawan Festival?

Balut

Lechon

Halo-Halo

Turon

Green Mango

Puto

Some trivia about the famous Filipino food you've just found...

	Puto	Puto is a sweet, savory steamed cake made of fermented rice flour
	Turon	Like a sweet spring roll - turon is made of bananas wrapped in spring roll wrapper and fried
	Green Mango	Philippine mangoes are famous for their distinct sweetness. But, they are also famously eaten sour, unripe (green) with bagoong (shrimp paste)
	Lechon	Whole roasted pig (lechon) is one of the most popular dishes in the Philippines. They are often stuffed with herbs and served with liver sauce.
	Halo-Halo	This dessert is a colorful mix of ingredients (hence the name "halo-halo" - meaning "mixed up"). Ingredients include shaved ice, flan, ube, beans, milk, ice cream, and more
	Balut	Balut is a famous Filipino delicacy made of boiled fertilized duck egg

MASSKARA

MassKara is an annual festival that takes place every October in Bacolod. The name comes from combining the words "mass" (meaning very many people), and "cara" (a Spanish word meaning "face"). Together they mean "a multitude of faces" It is also related to the word "maskara" - which, in Filipino, means "mask."

Bacolod is known as the "City of Smiles", so MassKara celebrates this with dances, parades, and parties featuring local food, arts, culture, music, and many talented performers in colorful costumes, and smiling masks.

Can you find these famous Filipinos in this multitude of smiles?

 Jose Rizal

 Agueda Kahabagan

 Melchora Aquino

Gregorio Del Pilar

Gabriela Silang

Apolinario Mabini

Some trivia about the Filipino heroes and historical figures you've just found...

	Jose Rizal	Jose Rizal is the National Hero of the Philippines. He was a scholar, writer, and had many other talents. His books were instrumental in inspiring leaders of the Philippine Revolution, and remain classics today.
	Agueda Kahabagan	Agueda was known to all as "Henerala Agueda." She was a leader, and general fighting for the freedom of the Philippines at the end of the 300+ year Spanish colonization.
	Melchora Aquino	Known as "Tandang Sora", Melchora Aquino is an icon of the Philippine Revolution. They called her the "Grand Woman of the Revolution, as she fed, supported, and treated Filipino soldiers from her store.
	Gregorio Del Pilar	Del Pilar was one of the youngest generals in the Philippine revolutionary army. Many referred to him as "Ang Batang Heneral" / "The Young/Boy General."
	Gabriela Silang	Gabriela Silang was also a revolutionary war hero. She was known as the leader of the movement in Ilocos, fighting for freedom from Spain.
	Apolinario Mabini	Apolinario Mabini was the first Prime Minister of the First Republic of the Philippines. He was a lawyer, and scholar. He was also differently-abled - requiring a wheelchair due to paralysis caused by polio

HIGANTES

The Higantes Festival happens every year in Angono, Rizal. It is mostly made up of a parade of giant papier-mâché puppets.

The parade is a celebration of the Feast of Saint Clement, and it is also said that it was once a form of protest against wealthy Spanish land owners in the area.

There are many different stories about the origins of the festival - some say it began in the Spanish era to quietly poke fun at, and protest against, the Spanish rule. Others say that it began after the 2nd World War.

Whatever its origins, today, the festival honors local government officials, the different barangays, and Angono's own folk tales.

Before the Spanish came, the Filipinos had their own ancient script. It was called Baybayin. Can you find some of these ancient characters hiding among the giants at the Higantes Festival?

= A

= DA

= BA

= GA

= KA

= PA

Some facts about the Baybayin system of writing...

Baybayin is an Ancient Filipino Script, used by early settlers and indigenous Filipinos before the Spaniards came to occupy the land. The script is made up of shapes and symbols used much like an alphabet - each symbol representing a sound.

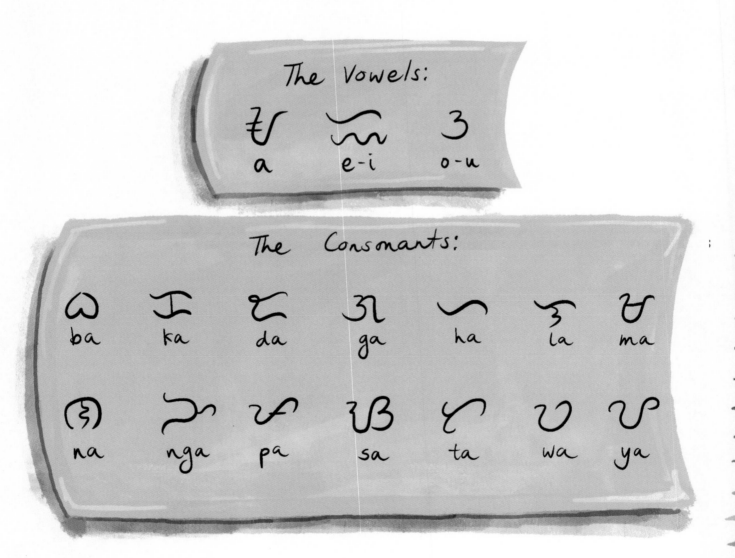

PASKO

The Philippines is a predominantly Catholic and Christian country, and so both for religious and cultural reasons, the Christmas season is like one, big, long festival! All across the Philippines, it is celebrated in different ways. In Pampanga, the Giant Lantern Festival happens every year in mid-December. At this festival, the Philippines' famous parols (hand-made, colorful lanterns, usually in the shape of stars) are on full, festive display.

In malls and shopping centers all over the country, Christmas trees and other decorations are put up. In Makati City, the Ayala Triangle puts in an impressive Christmas light show. And all across the country Filipinos engage in other traditions such as Simbang Gabi (midnight mass), and Noche Buena (the special family-focused Christmas Eve feast)

Can you find these Filipino Christmas classics in this Noche Buena scene?

 a green parol

 10 capiz lanterns

 a Nativity scene

 a church

 bibingka and puto bumbong

 tsokolate

Some information about the things you've just found...

	a green parol	"Parols" are colorful, star-shaped hand-made lanterns. They are used as Christmas decoration
	capiz lanterns	Capiz, also known as "Mother of Pearl" shell) is often used to make windows, lanterns, jewelry, and more.
	a Nativity scene	A Nativity Scene (also known as a "belen") is a scale model of the birth of Jesus Christ. Many Filipinos display one during Christmas.
	a church	Many Filipinos are Catholic. During Christmas season, they attend church daily for Simbang Gabi (Midnight Mass)
	bibingka and puto bumbong	Bibingka and puto bumbong are desserts often eaten at Christmas. Bibingka is steamed cake, Puto Bumbong is steamed sweet rice.
	tsokolate	During Noche Buena on Christmas Eve or Day, Filipinos have a hot cup of locally grown "tsokolate" (deep, dark, rich hot cocoa) with pastries

We hope you enjoyed your journey through these Filipino Festivals!

Find more books like this from KADO!

About the Author

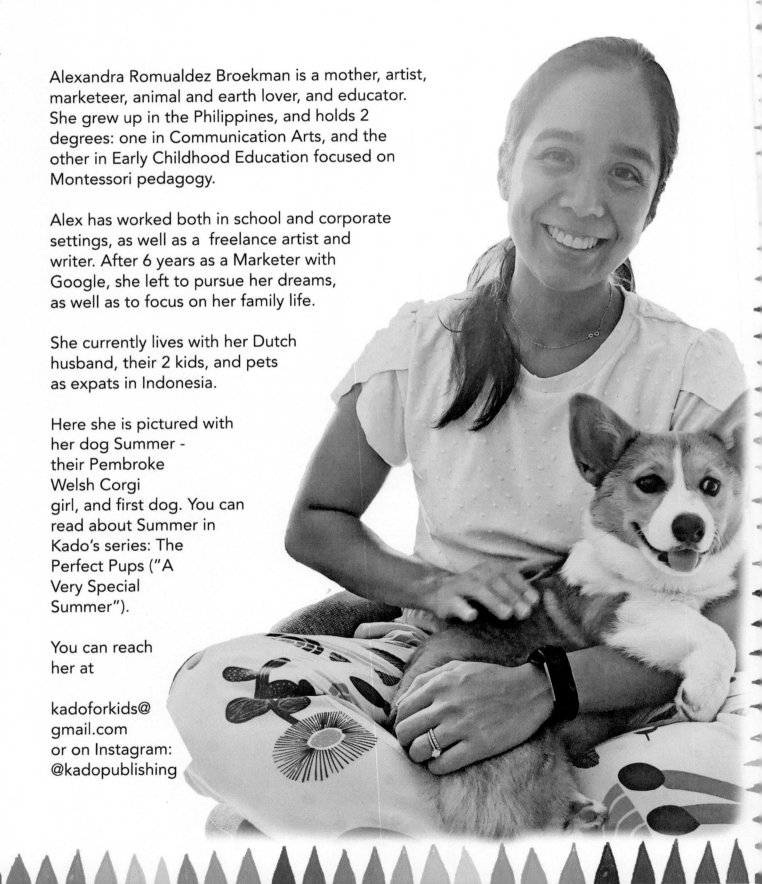

Alexandra Romualdez Broekman is a mother, artist, marketeer, animal and earth lover, and educator. She grew up in the Philippines, and holds 2 degrees: one in Communication Arts, and the other in Early Childhood Education focused on Montessori pedagogy.

Alex has worked both in school and corporate settings, as well as a freelance artist and writer. After 6 years as a Marketer with Google, she left to pursue her dreams, as well as to focus on her family life.

She currently lives with her Dutch husband, their 2 kids, and pets as expats in Indonesia.

Here she is pictured with her dog Summer - their Pembroke Welsh Corgi girl, and first dog. You can read about Summer in Kado's series: The Perfect Pups ("A Very Special Summer").

You can reach her at

kadoforkids@ gmail.com or on Instagram: @kadopublishing

find more
diverse, colorful
children's literature
through KADO!

Find us online at:

@kadopublishing on instagram
or Kado Publishing on the Kindle Store

This book is dedicated to Jay Broekman and his unending love and support.

We are also grateful for the below sources of our research for this book.

Events and Holidays - GOV.PH (2020). Gov.Ph. https//www.gov.ph/events-and-holidays

Muzones, G. (2020, September 23). 11 Best Festivals to Join in the Philippines. Guide to the Philippines. https://guidetothephilippines.ph/articles/history-culture/best-festivals-philippines

RedDoorz. "15 Philippines Festivals You Need To Experience." RedDoorz Blog, 29 Dec. 2020, www.reddoorz.com/blog/ph/places-to-visit-ph/15-philippines-festivals-you-need-to-experience.

Tourism Promotions Board. "Calendar of Philippine Festivals and Monthly Observances / Theme."
Tourism Promotions Board, 2018, www.tpb.gov.ph/tpb-calendar-of-promtions-and-marketing-activities/calendar-of-philippine-festivals-and-monthly-observances-theme.

Wikipedia contributors. (2020, November 28). List of festivals in the Philippines. Wikipedia. https://en.wikipedia.org/wiki/List_of_festivals_in_the_Philippines

If you liked this book, you may like other titles from this publisher...

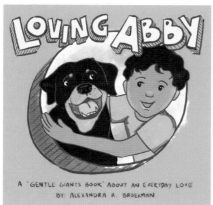

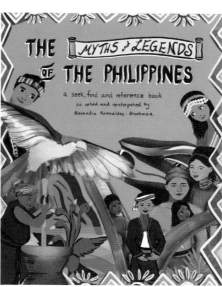

Shop all these and more!

Printed in Great Britain
by Amazon

10077297R00025